Preface

The artist-in-residence programme initiated by KfW Stiftung in cooperation with Künstlerhaus Bethanien serves as an incubator for artistic production, providing space for artists to pursue and shape their work, develop ideas, initiate new projects and perhaps try out different paths. The Brazilian-Indonesian artist Daniel Lie was invited to spend one year in Berlin under this programme to explore new horizons and engage in intercultural dialogue with peers and other cultural practitioners. This prompted Lie to test novel approaches. For the first time, the artist produced works on paper, using turmeric and charcoal to create expressive drawings.

Key themes in Daniel Lie's work are process, time and decay. The artist attempts to break with binary logic and reveals connections between ancestry and presence, rottenness and freshness, life and death. The artworks are often performative: organic materials such as plants, fungi, fabric, clay or soil combine to form large-scale installations that expand into space and react with it. The artist assumes the role of a collaborator, acting in conjunction with the material, the surrounding space and sometimes with other co-creators. Lie's approach regards art-making as closely connected with personal history, memory and life stories. During the one-year residency in Berlin, Lie focused and reflected on personal experiences as well as concepts of origin and identity.

This publication is a result of these ongoing reflections. Guided by Daniel Lie's artistic diaries, readers are invited to observe or even participate in that process. The book includes an interview with the Indonesian curator farid rakun that untangles concepts of collaboration and artistic agency. An essay by fellow artist, writer and curator Nomaduma Rosa Masilela offers an analysis of Lie's most recent drawings against the background of broader influences.

Daniela Leykam and Christoph Tannert
Editors

Contents

Quing, 2019

Death as expansion

The hegemonic construction of the human being can be understood as the relationship between the external and the internal of the body through senses and sensations. I have the impression that many people believe dying is the end of the sensible world: one no longer feels, all senses cease.

But what if it is the opposite? What if, at the precise moment we die, the senses begin to expand in a crescendo? What if we managed to amplify our sensorial cells, if the floor became an extension of our skin, the wall our ears, the ceiling our vision, the neighboring city our taste, if the smell of a distant continent invaded us, if we felt the touch of the deepest layer of the subsoil?

Death: not an end, but an expansion.

Lindinalva and the Balm, 2016

The Rangda cycle

The house of my Indonesian paternal grandparents in São Paulo was always treated as a sacred place. It was a large house, big enough for more than eleven members of the Lie family to reside in, and it contained several Indonesian memorabilia. These items always held an aesthetic fascination for me, which was enhanced by how closely they were guarded by my aunts.

When I was a child, I would be watched vigilantly whenever I touched one of these objects, and was even forbidden from entering some of the rooms – but this protective attitude only intensified the impression of sanctity. After the death of my grandfather, Lie Djoem Liem, the house was inhabited by one of my uncles until he passed away, too. Following these two deaths, the house stood shuttered and abandoned for two years and was finally sold.

Before it was handed over to the new owners, one of my aunts called a meeting of the whole family to rescue the valuables that might still be there. We met on the agreed day, 13 years ago. I had not been inside the house for over five years prior to that. Everything was in the same place, but time had left its mark: the walls had become moldy as a result of moisture; dust had settled on the furniture and objects, giving everything a grayish, homogeneous look; tree roots had gotten into the cracks; termites had infested the building, especially the library: when I opened a book, I could see paths and tunnels teeming with larvae among the pages.

To be there was a shock. We confronted all those sacralized spaces and objects that were once guarded with such vigilance and were now forgotten and decomposing. The house had transmuted into a ruin: it was rotting.

We spent a whole day there, engaged in a mixture of archaeological excavation and waste recycling. I felt as if I was plunging into a dense, humid, and thick darkness, and deep down I found a shiny object: a handmade silver pendant showing a face with a "scowl" – which I immediately related to the symbology of Indonesia.

That object became one of my most cherished treasures, which I carry with me until today. There was a time when I stopped taking it with me, two years ago, but that was interrupted by constant dreams in which I had the urge to find it; after an intense search, I have kept it close ever since.

Years later, I had the opportunity to ask my aunts if they knew to whom that pendant had belonged, but none of them were able to answer me – nor did they know what that object meant.

Later on I moved to Indonesia with the intention of getting to know and connecting with my ancestry. I had brought the pendant with me. I stayed in the city of Yogyakarta, a sultanate where the material heritage of humanity can be experienced at every corner. During that period, I visited the Prambanan temple, which is approximately 1,200 years old and still in use. It features several rooms dedicated to the various deities of Hinduism. I went there and meditated in each of them, but in a specific room – the one dedicated to the goddess Dewi Durga – I felt a more distinct energetic presence.

Two days later, I visited another temple: the Water Castle. In this temple, adorned with pastel-colored fresco decorations, I constantly saw the figure with the scowling face that I carry with me.

After these two visits I did a brief online search about the Indonesian Hindu deities and their meanings, and I found an image that corresponded to my scowling face – it was Dewi Durga/Rangda:

> *In Indonesia, the Hindu goddess Dewi Durga is symbolised as Rangda, a figure with long, dishevelled hair: her eyes were like twin suns, her mouth was like a cavern with protruding fangs, her two nostrils were like the holes of twin wells, and her entire skin was covered with spots and blemishes. She has a loyal following, who has given her the title of queen of spirits and ruler of the graves. The creepy form of Dewi Durga is considered a symbol of a woman's anger, and is enshrined in the form of the Rangda mask, which is sacred to the Balinese people until now.*[1]

By the time I realized that for the past thirteen years I had been carrying an image of an entity related to death, things came full circle. From the archaeological recycling experience at my grandparents' house – which was a milestone both in terms of my production as an artist and with regard to the development of my poetics – to the discovery of its meaning, I felt that I had always been relating to this deity, given that my artistic research has focused on possible nonbinary understandings of death.

Have I been in communion with Rangda all this time? An anachronistic, beyond-human communion?

1 Thomas M. Hunter and Ni Wayan Pasek Ariati, "Rangda in the Calon Arang: A Tale of Magic", in Michael Slouber (ed.), *A Garland of Forgotten Goddesses: Tales of the Feminine Divine from India and Beyond*, University of California Press: Oakland, 2021, pp. 217–243 (p. 234).

PODRERA, 2016

To Mourn the Living, detail, 2019

To remind us to be humble while not denying our agency

A conversation between farid rakun and Daniel Lie

This printed conversation is based on two exchanges between Daniel Lie and farid rakun in March and May 2021. Based on mutual interests such as other-than-human agency and collective work, farid was invited to a conversation that ultimately presented an opportunity to acknowledge how getting to know each other had impacted Daniel's artistic trajectory. In between the two online meetings, Daniel had to learn about the sudden death of their Indonesian father, who had immigrated to Brazil in 1959 and who tragically died of COVID-19. The conversation therefore delves deeper into cultural perspectives on death and loss, while connecting them to core elements of Lie's practice.

farid rakun: It was a very specific moment in my life when we met for the first time in São Paulo. It was in the second half of 2013, and I decided to come back to Indonesia after finishing my masters in the United States. "Okay," I thought, "I'm not going anywhere else, I'm going to return home to Jakarta to be with ruangrupa". I couldn't find anything like our collective anywhere else, and I also became aware that a lot of people were actually interested in Jakarta and Indonesia, and because my roots were in Jakarta it made sense to come back at that moment. It was during that time, while we were doing the 31st São Paulo Biennial, that I had my deepest involvement with ruangrupa. I think it was on one of those preliminary visits, and not only for me, but for a lot of us in ruangrupa, the people we met in Brazil left a lasting impression on us – which remains up until today.

Although we don't speak each other's languages – and not all Indonesians and Brazilians can speak English – I think we felt a strong connection. I don't know why, but with you, from what I remember, it was striking to find someone who had Indonesian blood running in their veins and who was interested in this heritage – although at that moment I don't think you had any deep knowledge about Indonesia and hadn't found a way yet to relate to the country as a part of your history, your family history and biography – the way you did things, how you approached them, your interests, everything seemed to me like you were planting seeds, metaphorically speaking. We've always been interested in that context, and you were a big part of that experience – at least subjectively. I remember visiting one of your studios at a residency, where I saw a glimpse of your work, and there was potential, talent, a distinct voice. I realised that it was something valuable, but I didn't know how to move on from there, and maybe up until now I still don't know why or how I would translate that interest, also because we haven't had the opportunity to work together in a professional way other than sharing networks.

Daniel Lie: How old were you at that time?

fr: I was turning 32.

DL: Ah, so you were the age I am now. That's very interesting, because you spoke about some decisions that relate to the ones I'm making right now: you finished something and then you had to decide where you were going and what to focus your energy on. At that time, I was leaving a collective I was organising parties with, and I was starting to feel the need to work with other structures and other people, which I found in the cultural institute Casa do Povo. Casa do Povo wasn't strictly a collective, but it was collective work; the environment was highly fertile, and it was during this period that I became motivated to start my own practice. In 2014, I began collaborating with art institutions, and since you were talking about seeds, I think that was a moment of germination for me: it had the strength of a sprout growing out of the earth.

Getting to know ruangrupa was very special, because you were the first Indonesians I met that were not immigrants – while I was growing up, there were no other Indonesians to interact with in our neighbourhood – and it felt like the first possibility to start engaging with this very close and yet distant universe that Indonesia had always been for me. Up until then, it had been only present through stories told by my family in my childhood. It was also important for me to start seeing myself from a cultural perspective as not fully Brazilian. Later on, in 2017, I was able to go to Indonesia for the first time to participate in the Yogyakarta Biennale, and we all met again. If our first encounter was like an introduction, then being in Indonesia for two months was perhaps the first chapter of a story – which was decisive for me, as I realised that I really needed to be there for a longer time, to research and to learn the language that was entwined with the culture. In 2019, I moved to Yogya for 14 months, and that was a very important experience for me. Very subtle things, which since my

Human Supremacy: The failed project, detail, 2019

first visit I'd been calling a "DNA memory", became more palpable and started to be connected with things from my past in a way that I didn't expect. While I was there, I also perceived how diverse it was – and that made me realise a lot of things about Brazil. When I was about to leave, I really felt a sense of home in Yogya, which I had never really felt in São Paulo – probably because my father was an immigrant and my mum was a migrant, and São Paulo is also a very tough city – but I had this feeling of home, I really felt connected to the geography, to the land. I recognised myself, and I'm still in the process of understanding what that means.

(nine weeks later)

DL: In these past three weeks, going through the process of mourning the death of my father, all these impressions have become even stronger.
In a way, it makes me realise the real reason for going to Indonesia: it was very much about taking a longer journey to get closer to my father, as well as to all the subjects that I'm interested in studying, such as the rituals and concepts related to death and the multiplicity of ways to understand it – and with all that, it was also about getting to know myself.

Now that this situation is so immediate and urgent and painful, I feel that my critique and my senses are agitated. It's been hard to do basic human things like eating, going to the bathroom, waking up or sleeping. At the same time, I've immersed myself in all the subjects and concepts that I've been researching or creating, because they are even more present now.
This might be a good moment to discuss this otherness, these entities we share a common interest in.

fr: I especially think about otherness, the other-than-human, as a good approach, as it has a capacity to remind us to be humble, while not denying our agency as humans. Unfortunately, I cannot overcome my limitations as a human being, for instance the fact that I only perceive the three-dimensional world through my senses. But, at least in my experience, this understanding of the other in the sense of inclusivity, even human to human, is inadequate, because it implies that being included, or rather being empowered, is something that comes from a powerful side and includes me, and therefore I should be thankful – and this is not enough. If we extend this line of thought to non-humans, it means we become aloof. That's how I would like to approach non-human entities: being very aware of our – or my – own limitations, and being humble as well. Because maybe, at the end of the day, our agency is not that important.

DL: These terms regarding otherness are also something I've been thinking about. If we say non-human, it goes back to this question of power relations, as in "who are we to diminish others' experiences", while the

PODRERA, detail, 2016

Death Center for the Living, 2017

concept of other-than-human[1] can be an attempt to make it more horizontal instead. In São Paulo, I could see a lot of dehumanisation as part of the social ideologies that are very present there, such as classism, xenophobia, prejudices based on gender, sexuality, race and so on – and that's why I ask myself: how can I talk about other-than-humans and look at other beings with the same perspective or as having the same rights as humans when I come from a context where even humans are not humanised? By looking at and trying to treat other beings with the same respect or in the same way I treat other humans, does that make me question my own humanity? Does that make me question my own limits?

COVID-19, for instance, a virus that is affecting the whole world, is an other-than-human. Since my father was killed by this other-than-human, it also makes me think about us as animals who are trying to survive in the world – and of course there are political issues around this, as he could already have been vaccinated. But to me it also has a wider meaning: a virus – an other-than-human – did this to my father; and the moment my father died he himself became an other-than-human: an ancestor.

Even with the global pandemic, with lots and lots of people dying, I feel how much the condition of dying – which should be like eating or sleeping – is completely marginalised and not integrated into daily life, at least in the western world or in Brazil; there is still a huge denial of it.

Talking about food, for instance, is something we often do with strangers: feeding oneself is a human need that is completely integrated into our lives. But when it comes to death, I feel there is a huge hypocrisy, not only in the way we talk about it, but also in the way we deal with it on a symbolical level – and it makes what I'm going through right now much harder.

1 Cf. Eduardo Kohn, *How Forests Think – Toward an Anthropology Beyond the Human*, University of California Press: Berkeley, 2013.

To Mourn the Living, detail, 2019

Death has become taboo. But how can something which is a certainty be turned into a taboo? If our society, at least in many parts of the world, didn't treat it as a taboo, I wonder if I would be experiencing the mourning differently, and if my life would be different. For many years I thought about how long I wanted to live, what would be the limit of my lifespan, and I would think I wanted to get very old, maybe a hundred. But as I continued to observe people who are very old, I started to think about the opposite: how do I want to die, and what do I need to do to die a good death?

fr: And I think it's very hard to define a standard of how to live properly, how to die properly, what to do with life, how to deal with the dying; we even build norms around things like that – as if they had become easier or more predictable to deal with, or more deliberate – but I think everyone should be able to deal with these things in their own way. And since you mention collectives: our lives, like our bodies, are our own; it's not about where it belongs, but belonging also affects other people. We can do almost anything – not really, not legally, like we cannot kill ourselves, for example – but legally or culturally or through religion we are being controlled in one way or another. So normalizing it, or turning something into norms, is often exactly where the problem lies – and of course it's a double-edged sword: the problem lies there because we're also social beings, and we are also part of something bigger.

DL: I wonder if we had normal conversations, acts or symbological representations with regard to death since childhood, the experience of dealing with it would be different – because this is also the thing about death and dying: we are always dealing with the death of others, and recreating rituals and experiences around it. Our own death is a very individual experience, and that's also the most interesting aspect: because it's so individual and so personal, it becomes a complete mystery, and maybe that's where a lot of the spiritual vision, religion, science and theory comes from, because there is no definite answer to it. There are many theories – but there's still something very wrong about this whole situation: it's hypocritical and overbearing to think that we humans are eternal, that we are the lords of this planet and that everything else is at our service. I think the crisis of civilisation that we are going through revolves around very basic things: our relationship with the world, our relationship with others, our respect for the planet and how we build these relationships. Of course, it's also an outcome of several technologies that create and maintain power structures – we would have to talk about colonisation, gender and race – but what I'm going through right now is really basic, and is everything at the same time. It's very powerful, it's very destructive, it's very beautiful, it's horrible, it's normal ... and it's confusing.

(Silence)
(Song/chant playing)

DL: But in a way, the question is also "how to stay". Because when someone who we are really a part of passes away and ceases to be present as a human being, we who stay behind, how do we keep on staying? I think this goes back to the bottom line of collectivity: the question of "how can we stay together?" and the importance of humbleness when we are working together, so that it doesn't destroy this force of staying.

fr: On that note, I think what's important for collectives, at least in my experience with collectives right now, is that instead of imagining that it will exist forever, it's actually also good to die a good death, as you said.

To Mourn the Living, detail, 2019

Umbral, detail, 2018

We are currently working on an initiative called "Manual for the dying", which is designed as a celebration of death. I think the death of a collective, or "collective death", when it has been properly prepared and is then celebrated, is actually the way, or a way, to go. The initiative is still in the making, but it's related to archiving and those acts that you performed in *Toko Buko Liong* (2020)[2], for example, addressing the question of how to archive the present, so that it's not only a form of salvage, but also paving the way, on a political level, for a good death.

DL: With *Toko Buko Liong* I started bringing together different perspectives on something that is pushed to the margin. I used the power of images, pre-images, concepts, and thought about how to put it together. Everybody has some sort of archive: objects, memories, pictures – ephemeral or not – but the thing about *Toko Buko Liong* was how to organise it in an emotional way. Often, archiving can be something very cold and distant, unrelated to the senses and to feelings. The challenge for me was to do this kind of organisation with emotions, with care, and also to approach the project in this way. I think it was very important to add an artistic and poetic dimension to it, not only data and historical facts. And I think I needed some kind of honesty, because the idea of dying is quite abstract. If I ask myself how I want to achieve a good death, I need to think about what is relevant and what are the bigger objectives in my life, not only in terms of work, but also in terms of what I want to build, construct, and see happen, so that I can peacefully say to myself "ok, *sudah*[3], enough"; for me it's more about how I can die in peace.

I've seen many people die without peace, and apart from the consequences for their afterlife in a spiritual sense, the fact that they didn't die in peace made things difficult for the people who stayed behind.

So that's also what I think you were talking about when you mentioned the "Manual for the dying": "ok, then how do we have to live in order to come to a conclusion one day?" It's important to have an initial agreement, so that one day when there is the need for an ending and for closure we can go back to that. Not to mention that even when we do have an agreement like this, it's already hard, depending on how we close things. But I specifically think that it's about denial, the tendency that we don't want to deal with it: I'm not going to face up to the fact that things are dying, I'm not going to deal with the fact that the end exists, that death is there, that if we start a project it's important to conclude it, that if we create something it's important to understand that one day it will cease to exist. I'm talking about how to confront this ending, and that's exactly where I think the hypocrisy lies: when we constantly think that things are not going to end, that the resources and our lives on this planet are unlimited and unchangeable, that our relationships will not one day come to end. Because that is what I feel and experience on many levels in this current state of mourning, that there is a sort of continuation – what do I do after the end? When it happens, it's going to be destructive, but do things really end? My father has become an other-than-human, he's expanding, his body is decaying right now in the grave; fungi and bacteria are decomposing his flesh and he's being transformed into air, into soil, so there are other living beings with him, with that body that has memory, disintegrating, transforming, expanding.

2 *Toko Buku Liong* (Liong Bookstore) is a collaborative art project by curator Adelina Luft (Romania/Indonesia) and artist Daniel Lie (Brazil/Indonesia) hosted online by Cemeti Institute for Art and Society from August 4 to September 4, 2020. The project is a joint effort to link the biographical fragments of the Lie family and the comics they produced and published at *Toko Buku Liong* in the 1950s by creating an affective archive situated at the intersection of identity politics, power structures and cultural agency in post-independence Indonesia. Divided into four volumes presenting artworks, essays and archival materials, the project shows an alternative route to mainstream history and intends to generate further conversations about authorship, subjectivities and the role of Indonesian comics in the construction of cultural identity. See: https://tokobukuliong.com/.

3 *Sudah* can mean "done" in Indonesian.

Death Center for the Living, 2017

Harvesting flowers in the sea

The Indonesian island of Java has its own way of measuring time. In the Javanese calendar there is a specific date called Malam Jumat Kliwon (Friday Night Kliwon). On one of those dates, January 9, 2020, my Indonesian colleagues told me what it meant: this day was dedicated to praying and honoring the dead and the spirits. Folklore has it that on the night of Kliwon spirits are more present and can perform actions (many tales surrounding this date are horror stories).

Upon hearing about this celebration and seeing people lighting incense sticks in the cemetery in front of my house, I called a friend from Ecuador who was also staying in Yogyakarta. That night, we rode our motorcycles to Pantai Parangkusumo Beach, which was 25 minutes away from my house.

On this beach there is a temple to the Javanese queen of the sea, Nyai Roro Kidul, which was built around a large volcanic rock. Mysteriously, the nearest volcano is 50 km away.

It was full moon and the smell of incense was pervasive despite the constant strong wind. The sea was very rough – it was always dangerous to swim there. Several people were sitting and some were standing looking at the sea, letting the waves wash around their feet a few times and touching the water with the palms of their hands and bringing it to their faces.

We made our offerings and had our moment of prayer. Meanwhile, several people with lighted lanterns were walking around looking for something. At first, I thought they were fishing for small crustaceans in the wet sand – it reminded me of the practice of fishing for shrimp with lanterns at night in Brazil.

We asked one person what these people were doing, and they told us:

"They are harvesting the flower petals washed up by the sea. During the day, people come and make offerings to the waves – and many people offer flowers. The sea takes them and returns some of the petals. These returned petals are used later in other offerings, or are left by people in their homes."

For me, the beauty of this description lies in the interaction between humans, spiritual beings, plants, and the sea. In this relationship, the sea carries the petals back to the beach as a blessing and response to the communication previously established in the act of offering. However, in being returned, the energetic value of the petals is increased or changed – because it has been blessed / energized / anointed / baptized / magnetized with another sort of power.

Our communication with spiritual or beyond-human beings is performed in the only way we know, using the human habit: we offer them things that are intrinsically ours – such as food or drink, perfumes or flowers, meat or vegetables – all that is primarily needed and appreciated by humans. We afford these beings the same care as for human lives.

Human Supremacy: The failed project, 2019

Human Supremacy: The failed project, 2019

Crying as a portal

In navigating the memories of strong feelings, we sometimes get to a point where the same emotion of those moments can bring tears to our eyes – like walking down a corridor that leads us to a door, and that door makes us travel back in time. By crying and reliving the feeling, we are there again and can break the order of space and time.

My grandmother from Pernambuco arrives at her husband's funeral at the Quarta Parada cemetery in eastern São Paulo propped up on either side by one of her grandsons to help her walk. Instead of using a walker, the matriarch relies on her offspring, and as she approaches the coffin she is communing with Grandpa Miguel's body.

At the funeral of my Indonesian grandfather, my aunt breaks the silence when the coffin is lowered into the ground by playing a farewell song with her harmonica.

My friend reads a farewell text to his father in English, and the very moment he starts reading it begins to rain; as soon as he has finished, the rain stops.

At daybreak, as we leave Pappie's funeral, a comet appears in the sky on the horizon; my father, who is driving, says that this is his father's final goodbye.

I find Nina's body – the same one I chose when she was a newborn 15 years ago. Her body is hard, lying on a chrome table; I take her old blanket and some adhesive tape and wrap her up, making a cocoon.

A dog attacks a cat that strays into my yard. I can't see what is happening because it is dark. I pour water on the two and manage to stop them fighting. I go to see how the cat is; severely wounded, it looks at me and meows tenderly. I leave, and when I come back it is already dead. Our neighbor, the owner, takes its body away inside a banana leaf.

A great-grandmother goes to mourn her great-granddaughter's body. She is over a hundred years old, but even after having reached such old age, something only a few people manage, she is still vulnerable to the cruelties of the world and has to grieve for the daughter of her daughter's daughter – between the wrinkles, her gaze is one of pain.

According to the Jewish tradition, you do not open a coffin at the funeral wake. I could not really understand that, maybe because it was my first wake and I was only ten years old. My brother gets annoyed with my behavior and calls out to me. When the body is buried, each person at the funeral has to throw a handful of earth and a flower onto the coffin; in the process, my aunt, recently widowed, hugs me and we cry – I understand.

At the cemetery, after carrying and burying the coffin of Grandpa Miguel, I stay for a moment in solitude at his grave. I see an apparition: a thin beam of light begins to curve and forms a perfect circle.

Children of End, 2018

An existential scale of understanding: On fungus and fabulation in Daniel Lie's oeuvre

By Nomaduma Rosa Masilela

A moment of silence before we begin.

In a corner of Daniel Lie's studio at Künstlerhaus Bethanien sits a bowl filled with fruit and vegetables. Undisturbed, it quietly transforms as it slowly decays. The fruits gain fur, lose firmness, acquire a new turgidity and texture as they shrink in on themselves and cycle through the slow process of decomposition and decay.

As the fruits and vegetables decompose, Lie composes a series of mixed-media drawings on paper in response to the slow, evolving process of death, decay, and of artistic creation. Lie's oeuvre, which includes performances, illustrations and large-scale installations, reveals the many ways in which creating follows a process of fabulation similar to that of decay.

A pastel and watercolour field of green and yellow serves as the background for a scattered cacophony of charcoal shapes, both figurative and abstract. *Scales of Decay* (2020) is a large-format multimedia work on paper that hangs from the ceiling on a wooden rod, like a banner, a hanging sheet, or a reinvented "jammer". The work depicts a bowl of decomposing fruit exploded across the picture plane – a détournement of the core elements of a traditional still-life painting through a combination of dynamism, incompleteness, and a flurry of gesture and movement. Lie's détournement of still-life stasis reflects a core philosophy of their practice which engages the decayed and rotten as expansive vectors through which to critically fabulate processes of life and death, loss and existence, narrative and enunciation, both within the experiences of human life and within those which Lie calls "other-than-human".

Is silence an absence?

While on residency and living in Indonesia for an extended period of time for the first time in their life, Lie learned of the power of silence, which they described as not simply an absence of noise, but as another form of communication with matter. During this time, acclimatising to an unfamiliar country that their ancestors had called home, Lie had to "access the power of a specific silence. [...] Living here has been a process of rebirth, [...] to develop a new form of accessing my body."[1] The rebirth that Lie experienced during their year in Indonesia was also fuelled by an online art and archival project which explored the history of their grandparents, who emigrated to Brazil from Indonesia in 1958. Titled *Toko Buku Liong* (2020), the project was web-hosted by the Cemeti Institute for Art and Society, and was a collaboration between Lie and curator Adelina Luft. It operated as an effort to put together the biographical fragments of Lie's family history before their immigration to Brazil and the archival remnants of the comic books that their grandparents produced through their family-run bookstore in Semarang, Indonesia, in the 1950s.[2] Combining personal narratives, artworks, as well as historical and archival research, the project was an affective archive that served as a "strategy to recover my Indonesian roots, undernourished due to 60 years of migration and 17,790 kilometres of distance".[3]

Toko Buku Liong unfolded over four multilingual and multimedia chapters, operating as an exhibition, publication and artwork which proposed an "alternative route from mainstream history and hope[d] to further generate conversations on authorship, subjectivities, and the role of Indonesian comics in the construction of a cultural identity".[4] Lie's grandparents Lie Djoen Liem and Ong King Nio ran the Liong Bookstore throughout the 1950s, when the newly independent nation was forging a cohesive identity. A number of new and specifically modern forms of culture emerged in Indonesia and were popularised in the service of articulating a sense of nationhood – comic books in particular played an important role in shaping postcolonial subjectivity in both Indonesia and numerous other newly independent countries in the mid-twentieth century. Curator Okwui Enwezor wrote about the socio-political importance of comic books in independent African nations, describing them as "sites of subjectivity because they are symbols and signs for collective public speech" and concluding that "the comics are fundamentally embedded in the discursive and political structures that make new publics and counter-publics simultaneously".[5]

1 Daniel Lie, Juliana Dos Santos, "60 years of migration and 17,790 kilometers away", in *Terremoto*, Issue 19: *Planetary Solidarity – Ancestrality*. November 3, 2020 (https://terremoto.mx/en/revista/60-anos-de-migracion-y-17-790-kilometros-de-distancia/, last accessed: May 19, 2021). Text translated from Spanish to English by Isabel Ruíz.

2 *Toko Buku Liong*, web-hosted by Cemeti Institute for Art and Society, Yogyakarta, Indonesia (August 4 – September 4, 2020) (https://tokobukuliong.com).

3 Daniel Lie, Juliana Dos Santos.

4 *Toko Buku Liong*.

5 Okwui Enwezor, "Rapport des forces: African comics and their publics", in *Africa Comics* (on the occasion of the exhibition *Africa Comics*, The Studio Museum in Harlem, New York, November 15, 2006 – March 18, 2007). New York: The Studio Museum in Harlem, 2006, pp. 18–19.

Scales of Decay, 2021

Matriarch's Enigma, 2021

While comics shaped public opinion, they were also reflections of political schisms and contention. The *Wiro, Anak Rimba Indonesia* comic series that Lie's grandparents produced in 1957–58 (illustrated by Kwik Ing Hoo) chronicled the Tarzan-like adventures of a fair-skinned, Java-born teenage boy named Wiro. All of the ten volumes were conservative in their representations of racial and gender relations (i.e. patriarchal and imperialist), but this aspect possibly served as a veil to hide the producers' own increasing precarity and estrangement within an Indonesian national identity whose cohesion was predicated upon exclusion. As Lie explains: "Back then, comics were as influential as social media is today. In the process of creation of a new national identity, they purposefully excluded those of Chinese descent, like my family. It is ironic to think that the work that my ancestors created also reproduced the ideology that excluded them."[6] Enwezor writes of similar fears (and realities) of political repression within comic production in colonial and postcolonial Africa, stating that "repression can force speech to strangle the speaker literally, because such a mode of expression can be taken as an excess of speech, as speech that exceeds the limits of its tolerability."[7]

In a way, Lie applies a principle of excess to his own oeuvre, such as in the large-scale drawing *Micro/Macro* (2020). The work on paper is an expansive efflorescence of movement and colour resisting any stable orientation; some white markings appear to delineate a form, while others appear to hover on the picture plane, referencing not only the decay of the central form represented, but the possibility of the eventual decay of its substrate, the paper. This double decay recalls scholar Achille Mbembe's theorisation on the double nature of the image in Cameroonian comics, which has the "ability to annex and mime what it represents, while, in the very act of representation, masking the power of its own arbitrariness, its own potential for opacity, simulacrum and distortion."[8] With *Micro/Macro*, Lie adopts the visual language of comics and expands it beyond the storyboard field of representation and into the experiential and somatic register of affect, similar to an earlier series of illustrations Lie produced for their *Toko Buku Liong* project, which reimagined a more politically complex and multivalent afterlife for the character in their grandparents' comic book. One such work, *Wiro and the consequences of patriarchy* (2020), offers a more metaphysical and affective narrative for Wiro that moves beyond the patriarchal, monocultural and exclusionary binaries imposed by the government and represented within the original Wiro comics.[9] These works reflect Lie's interest in the scalar relationship between personal cosmologies and greater historical/experiential phenomena. Similarly, *Micro/Macro* and *Scales of Decay* are simply representations of objects rotting in a studio in Berlin as well as critical fabulations of existential quandaries.

Is absence a loss?

The cacophony of forms swirling around the central composition in *Scales of Decay* appear as though lost at sea, recalling the multilayered works of artist Ellen Gallagher, whose paintings similarly deploy a combination of abstracted representations of microscopic (sea) organisms and clear figuration to examine the complicated relationship between epistemology and power in narratives of the Middle Passage as well as to mark the immeasurable loss of life and memory caused by the Atlantic slave trade.[10] Quite obviously, Lie and Gallagher do not share the same subject-matter; however, they share a similar concern for plumbing the depths of

6 Daniel Lie, Juliana Dos Santos.

7 Enwezor, p. 19.

8 Achille Mbembe, "Chapter 4: The thing and its double", in *On the Postcolony*. Berkeley and Los Angeles, California: University of California Press, 2001, p. 142.

9 These works can be found in "Jilid/Chapter IV: The specters of Wiro" of the *Toko Buku Liong* project (https://tokobukuliong.com/the-specters-of-wiro/uncle-wiro/).

10 See Ellen Gallagher's series *Watery Ecstatic* (2001–ongoing) and the work *Bird in Hand* (2006).

lost, unacknowledged and erased histories and sensibilities, which requires a narrative-making methodology like "critical fabulation", a concept developed by scholar Saidiya Hartman. In response to the innumerable erasures of Black women within the archives that chronicle the Middle Passage, and with an acknowledged need for the construction of a narrative in the face of such profound epistemological and human loss, Hartman proposes a method which centres on speculative and subjective arguments in order to construct a narrative which can exceed the bounds of a traditional archive that is predicated on maintaining the inequities of power which constituted its existence in the first place, as well as one which "can embody life in words and at the same time respect what it cannot know".[11]

Toko Buku Liong was such an attempt, a concrete effort to create an affective archive mining the "countless *might-have-beens*" of "*anachronism escombros [shadows]*" left through dislodged, marginalised and forgotten histories.[12] With this work, Lie and their collaborator were able to make narrative reparation by crediting their grandmother as a co-author of *Wiro*, as she had consistently been effaced from authorship.[13] There is a necessary and ethical imperative to this act of reparation; Hartman also reflects on the longing that such an erasure and loss engenders, and while she warns against certain actions which are simply about filling the void within the archive, she insists on "writing at the limit of the unspeakable and unknown" – a creative and historical methodology that is centred around the intention "both to tell an impossible story and to amplify the impossibility of its telling" in order to interrogate modes of knowledge production and assumed knowhows rather than attempt to replace that which has been lost.[14]

Through loss, a presence.

Daniel and I both lost our fathers in the past year. A dedication written in ghostly pencil along the back of *Scales of Decay* reads "In memory of Lie Liong Khing * 01/12/1957 – Semarang / Indonesia – 17/04/2021 São Paulo / Brazil", commemorating Lie's father. The work memorialises their father not only in this written line, but in the formal relationship of the work to the comic storyboard, which connects to an at least three-generation lineage of illustrators within the Lie family: "Since [the] passing of my father I remembered this memory [of] asking my father to draw a large-scale popular comic book character, he glues some pieces of paper carefully and sketched calmly and paying attention [...] – for me that was one of my first introductions [to] being an artist." At the same time, they also had a clear memory of the love felt by a child towards their parent.[15]

Micro/Macro visually represents the varying scales of existence – from the microscopic and singular to the expansive and cosmic. The work is based on a numerical tally of the exponentially increasing rate of the generational expansion of humans, which points to a central tenet of Lie's practice, which has been ongoing since at least 2008. In that year, he produced a drawing titled *Âmago* (English: core of one's being), which deployed a similarly abstracted microscopic mode. Another example is the collaborative performance created in 2018 with Juliana Dos Santos and Bruna Amaro titled *Ablution*, which drew on the Buddhist belief that we carry the lives of seven previous generations within us.[16]

11 Saidiya Hartman, "Venus in two acts", in *Small Axe* (2008) 12(2), p. 3.

12 Daniel Lie, Adelina Luft, "Jilid/Chapter I – Escombros". *Toko Buku Liong* website (https://tokobukuliong.com/escombros/).

13 "Daniel Lie on family, heritage, and the myth of origin", in *Sugar Nutmeg* podcast, by Ruth Feriningrum and Alexandra Kumala, recorded 02/04/2021, 1hr 38 min (https://play.acast.com/s/sugar-nutmeg/edbc6eaa-eb52-42e6-982f-b081abea6fd3, last accessed: May 21, 2021).

14 Hartman, pp. 1 and 11.

15 Private message from Daniel Lie to author, sent on Wednesday, May 5, 2021.

16 *Ablution* was performed by Daniel Lie, Bruna Amaro and Juliana Dos Santos on Saturday, April 28, 2018, at De Single, Belgium (https://desingel.be/en/programme/festivals/daniel-lie-bruna-amaro-juliana-dos-santos-ablution, last accessed: May 19, 2021).

Dife and Leath, 2021

After the arrival of the prophecy, detail, 2021

Rombo, 2021

Lie describes their time in Indonesia as one during which, "through searching for my ancestors' stories, I found my own story and the process of understanding lead to an existential scale of understanding".[17] This "existential scale of understanding" is not predicated solely on anthropocentrism, but based on the inextricable and rhizomatic relation between life and death. As Lie explains: "When we die we become part of a group of beings that I recognise as other-than-human. [...] When their bodies disintegrate, they expand in the world, in the same manner that all of our mothers and ancestors have disintegrated. The rock can be my ancestor as well as my great-grandmother."[18] Their work exposes our close relationship to other non-human beings, described by Thich Nhat Hahn as "interbeing", while also expanding the possibilities of a deeper relationship with the interrelated nature of life and death, and the cosmologies which frame our understanding of existence writ large. My own father, Dr. Ntongela Desmond Joseph Masilela (1948–2020) passed away from cancer; the same had befallen his father, and throughout much of my life I watched my father struggle with the impending possibility of a similar fate curtailing his life's work. In her *Cancer Journals*, the poet Audre Lorde writes of her own fight with cancer and her fear of death, highlighting the immense process of releasing herself from the European ideas of death as abjection or as a cancelling of existence, and arriving at a deeply considered relation that allowed for a vigour and life force to empower her energies – i.e. her life's work, regardless of how much time there is left to live. As she writes: "Yet once I face death as a life process, what is there possibly left for me to fear? Who can really have power over me again?"[19] In conversation with the writings of Hartman and numerous other Black radical thinkers, the sociologist Ruha Benjamin reflects about an alternate life force: "Yes, subordination, subjugation, subaltern, literally 'under the earth,' racialized populations are buried people. But there is a lot happening underground. Not only coffins, but seeds, roots and rhizomes. And maybe even tunnels and other lines of flight to new worlds, where alternative forms of kinship have room to grow and to nourish other life forms and ways of living."[20] This belief also guides Lie's practice, which addresses human and other-than-human realities. While Lie clearly is aware of the conceptual practices of artists who view art as shamanism, like Tunga and Joseph Beuys, they have been more ethically influenced by their mentor Mônica Nador, whose work focuses on building a sense of communion. The heart of Lie's practice and oeuvre thus far have been large-scale installations that viewers can enter and that engage with alternative forms of kinship and ways of living, such as *Death Center for the Living* (2017), which was presented at Performeum as part of the Wiener Festwochen.

Composed of soils, minerals, plants, rotting fruit, flowers and two centrally placed *Cannabis indica* plants, *Death Center for the Living* invited visitors to settle on straw mats and fully immerse themselves in the visual setting, the smell of fermenting rice in ceramic vases, and the sound of a deep base composition produced by the musician Vivian Caccuri.[21] It operated as a hybrid space of installation, performance and ritual site filled with invisible layers and fields of emotion evoking the rotten and decayed, allowing visitors to develop an altered relationship to the transience of time and to perceive death not only in terms of abjection and loss, but as a site of regeneration and possibility. A later installation presented at the 14th Yogyakarta Biennale, *Between a bless and a curse* (2017), further elaborated

17 Daniel Lie, Juliana Dos Santos.

18 Ibid. This concept can also be seen in an animated video of a poem by Lie, titled *The Ruins Are my Home (2020)*, in "Jilid/Chapter I", *Toko Buku Liong* website (https://tokobukuliong.com/escombros/the-ruins-are-my-home/).

19 Audre Lorde, "Breast cancer: power vs. prosthesis", in *The Cancer Journals*. London: Penguin Classics, 2020 (1980).

20 Ruha Benjamin, "Black AfterLives Matter: Cultivating kinfulness as reproductive justice", in *Making Kin Not Population* (eds. Clarke, Adele E. and Haraway, Donna). Chicago: Prickly Paradigm Press, 2018, p. 47.

21 Video documentation can be found online (https://www.youtube.com/watch?v=Nb7N6PO_HTs&t=220s).

the possibilities and tensions of communion and smell. This full-room immersive installation was composed of 127 ceramic vases filled with fungi and fermented rice along with other natural materials, forming several pyre-like structures throughout the room and creating an intense, possibly excessive olfactory geography for visitors. Its extreme effect illustrated that "smell is the presence of another in ourselves. Hard to describe, yet vivid, smell leads into encounter – and indeterminacy."[22]

... a field of emotion.

In deploying the fungi, bacteria, mushrooms and other beings in various stages of decay, Lie reimagines new possibilities inherent in the process of decomposition, such as creation and regeneration. As they point out, "in my experience it was very strong to understand that fungi are beyond life and death. This concept is very small for this entity."[23] Rather, Lie views fungi as incredible sources of power and energy, as exemplified by their solo show *The Negative Years* at Jupiter Artland, Scotland, staged in 2019 after more than two years of research. *Quing* (2019), part of a series of large installations, featured a biological heater that worked by mixing bacteria and fungi with straw, soil and manure and that served to heat water flowing in pipes through the installation room. This mechanism required the right temperature so that the pink oyster and winter oyster mushrooms and other "unnamed entities" in the installation could flourish.[24] Lie described the process of creation as a collaboration with "other-than-human" entities, including the fungi queendom, bacteria, plants, elements, spirits and deities. This work shows the energy potential of decomposition, not only in terms of the electric energy created, but also in terms of emotional energy: "We're using the word 'mystical' and I like to use the word 'energy' too, but we're talking about a certain type of energy. [...] maybe we can call this kind of energy a field of emotion. But these words are not enough."[25]

This brings us back to the necessity of excess, of speculation, of fabulation to overcome the limitations of cosmologies, politics and words that are not enough. When thinking about the frames of reference of this work, the aforementioned shamanic practices resonate both with the communion-focused work of Nador and with the traditions of art-making in the name of political and ethical liberation as practised by a number of Brazilian conceptual artists, in particular Lygia Pape, Hélio Oiticica and Cildo Meireles, who had consistently expanded the possibilities of artistic creation in resistance to political oppression. Working within and beyond this tradition, Lie adopts the ethics of understanding that "this expansion process is a process of liberation."[26] Lie points out that art institutions are often unable to contend with the living beings that their installations introduce, e. g. by exuding smells that offer a way to liberate viewer conventions within public museums.[27] In a similar act of expanding words that are not enough, Lie transforms the concepts of king and queen into something that is "neither-nor", queering the assumed binaries: "This is also the search for the experience of non-binary life, not only in the place of gender, but also to broaden that view and deal with life from a non-binary point of view. That is, looking at it in at least a third way. Then we expand to a fourth, fifth, sixth, seventh way."[28]

22 Anna Lowenhaupt Tsing, *The Mushroom at the End of the World: On the Possibility of Life in Capitalist Ruins*. New Jersey: Princeton University Press, 2015, p. 46.

23 Daniel Lie, Jonas Van, "Rotten pedagogies: exercises from the process of organic matter transition", in *Usure Presse* no. 1 (2020), pp. 20–26.

24 Further reading: Wong Binghao, Madeline Murphy Turner, Daniel Lie, "A version of reality: conversation with Daniel Lie", in *Post: Notes on Art in a Global Context*, MoMA (NY), June 23, 2021 (https://post.moma.org/a-version-of-reality-conversation-with-daniel-lie/, last accessed July 1, 2021).

25 Daniel Lie, Ross Simoni, "Interview with Daniel Lie", in *ArtReview*, March 15, 2018 (from the September 2017 issue of *ArtReview*, https://artreview.com/ar-september-2017-simonini-daniel-lie, last accessed May 19, 2021).

26 Daniel Lie, Jonas Van, "Rotten pedagogies: exercises from the process of organic matter transition", in *Usure Presse* no. 1 (2020), pp. 20–26.

27 This training is explained by Susan Cahan in "Visitor behavior", in *Felix Gonzalez-Torres*. New York: Art Resources Transfer, Inc., 1993.

28 Daniel Lie, Jonas Van, p. 23.

Micro/Macro, 2021

Busuk, 2021

This sharp awareness is also essential to a critical fabulation that exceeds the knowledge systems limiting our capacity for existence. A narrative reparation for the fungus, a means of communication with these other-beings, a politics of enunciation that goes beyond the postcolonial offer of a "third space" and explodes into multitudes of spaces, allowing for multiple lives and afterlives: "Is it possible that transitioning, like decolonizing, demands a form of care which is solvent, that is to say: a form of care which mediates the deterioration of things, which accompanies the duration of the ruin, which deepens the crack of the horizon, and which settles into lava the world of sense, formulae, figures, and oeuvres of power which any transition, just as any decolonizing process, demands to see burn."[29] This is not fast work, but rather slow, generous work of surrender, which recognises that the fungus queendom operates within its own process and logic. Lie's practice opposes stasis and does not desire to be concretely "known", as it refuses to systematise the beings and epistemologies that their work encounters, instead embracing their opacity.[30] At the same time, Lie emphasises the deliberate limited temporality of the work: at the end of exhibitions, Lie returns the soil and fungi and fermented matter back to nature as best they can. The ephemerality of the work does not negate its enduring resonance: "The ephemeral does not equal unmateriality. It is more nearly about another understanding of what matters."[31] As Lie concludes: "My challenge is to make something that one day will also have a life of its own, and its creation will be a contribution to this world, the very contributing being a rupture in the fog produced by heterosexual, patriarchal cisgenderism that insists on blinding us from the possibilities of a deeper relationship with existence."[32] Lie's latest large-scale installation, *Sopro (Sigh)* (2021), is a public outdoor sculpture commissioned by the Berlinische Galerie soon after the death of their father. Built as an expression of a process of grief and release, it has been left out in the open for a few months. Now, things begin to grow.

Dedicated to our fathers,
our mothers and us who survive them,
and the countless
other-than-human entities
that surround us
cacophonously.

29 Jota Mombaça, "For an ontological strike", in *We don't need another hero* (catalogue for the 10th Berlin Biennale for contemporary art). Germany: Distanz Verlag, 2018, p. 47.

30 See Edouard Glissant, "For opacity", in *Poetics of Relation*. Ann Arbor: University of Michigan Press, 1997.

31 José Esteban Muñoz, *Cruising Utopia: The Then and There of Queer Futurity*. New York and London: New York University Press, 2009, p. 81.

32 Daniel Lie, Juliana Dos Santos.

Scales of Decay, exhibition view, 2021

Âmago, 2008–2011

In loving memory of

Lie Liong Khing
Semarang, Indonesia, 1 December 1956 – São Paulo, Brazil, 27 April 2021

and

Lindinalva Melo Costa
Garanhuns, Brazil, 14 January 1921 – São Paulo, Brazil, 17 September 2020

Quing, 2019

List of images

Quing, pink oyster mushroom (*Pleurotus salmoneo-stramineus*), winter oyster mushroom (*Pleurotus ostreatus*), unnamed entities, turmeric and flaxseed gel paint, ceramic jars with rice, water and sugar, natural fibre rope, plastic sack, cotton fabric, biological digestion heater, copper pipe, mechanical pipe system, water, dimensions variable, exhibition views, *The Negative Years*, Jupiter Artland, Edinburgh, Scotland, 2019, photos: Ruth Clark, ©the artist

Lindinalva and the Balm, installation and performance with Daniel Lie and Lindinalva Melo da Costa, 90 green coconuts, metal chain, sisal ropes, lemongrass, snake plant, flowers and aloe vera, Bank of Brazil Cultural Center, São Paulo, Brazil, 2016, photo: Leonardo Matsuhei, ©the artist

PODRERA, hemp, ropes, fabric, hay, dead tree, cotton fabric, bananas and mud (dirt collected from the area, horse excrement, hay and linseeds), dimensions variable, installation view, PROJETO BRASIL – TROPICALYPSE NOW!, Kampnagel, Hamburg, Germany, 2016, photos: Martin Meiser, ©the artist

To Mourn the Living, detail, pink oyster mushroom (*Pleurotus salmoneo-stramineus*), unnamed entities, natural fibre rope, pulley, flowers, jute sack, rocks, charcoal, flaxseed gel paint, dimensions variable, installation view, *The Negative Years*, Jupiter Artland, Edinburgh, Scotland, 2019, photos: Ruth Clark, ©the artist

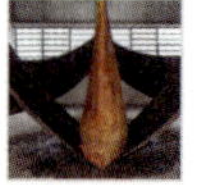
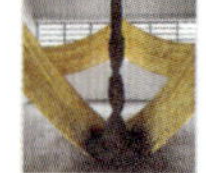

Human Supremacy: The failed project, jute fabric covered with mud and linseed, cotton fabric naturally dyed with turmeric, straw with fungi (*Lyophyllum shimeji*), ropes, dimensions variable, Casa do Povo, São Paulo, Brazil, 2019, photos: Edouard Fraipont, ©the artist

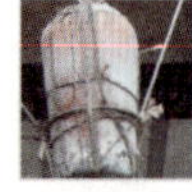

Umbral, 85 terracotta ceramic urns filled with organic matter, natural fibre rope and fungi, dimensions variable, detail, Valongo Festival, Santos, Brazil, 2018, photo: Daniel Lie, ©the artist

Death Center for the Living, dirt, straw, sprouting line, seeds, mud, hemp fabric, hemp ropes, rotten fruits, flowers, speaker boxes, ceramic vases, water, straw mats, 3 ceramic vases with fermenting rice inside and two *Cannabis indica* plants, in partnership with Vivian Caccuri (sound design and original music), approx. 10 x 14 x 11 m, installation view, Wiener Festwochen, Vienna, Austria 2017, photo: Daniel Lie, ©the artist

Children of End, flowers, jute fabric, hay, cotton fabric, 13 hanging batik paintings, sisal rope, ceramic jar with water (floor), ceramic jar with fungi, rice, coconut milk and water (hanging), mud (dirt, hay and linseeds), diverse foliage, wall painting with horizontal stripes, Casa Triângulo, São Paulo, Brazil, 2018, photo: Filipe Berndt, ©the artist

Scales of Decay, exhibition view, Künstlerhaus Bethanien, Berlin, Germany, 2021, photo: David Brandt, © Künstlerhaus Bethanien

Scales of Decay, charcoal, watercolour and soft pastel on paper, 200 x 165 cm, 2020, exhibition view, Künstlerhaus Bethanien, photo: David Brandt, © Künstlerhaus Bethanien

Matriarch's Enigma, ink, oil stick and soft pastel on paper, 310 x 150 cm, 2021, exhibition view, Künstlerhaus Bethanien, photo: David Brandt, © Künstlerhaus Bethanien

Dife and Leath, turmeric, linseed gel, linseeds, charcoal, oil stick, water colour, soft pastel on paper, 300 x 350 cm, 2021, exhibition view, Künstlerhaus Bethanien, Berlin, Germany, 2021, photo: David Brandt, © Künstlerhaus Bethanien

After the arrival of the prophecy, charcoal, watercolour, oil stick and soft pastel on paper, 160 x 150 cm, 2021, detail, photo: Daniel Lie, © the artist

Rombo, charcoal, watercolour, oil stick and soft pastel on paper, 200 x 165 cm, 2020, courtesy the artist, exhibition view, Künstlerhaus Bethanien, Berlin, Germany, 2021, photo: David Brandt, © Künstlerhaus Bethanien

Micro/Macro, charcoal, watercolour, oil stick and soft pastel on paper, 215 x 150 cm, 2020, courtesy the artist, exhibition view, Künstlerhaus Bethanien, photo: Daniel Lie, © the artist

Busuk, charcoal, watercolour and soft pastel on paper, 85 x 75 cm, 2021, exhibition view, Künstlerhaus Bethanien, 2021, photo: David Brandt, © Künstlerhaus Bethanien

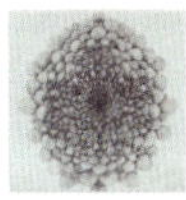

Âmago, drawing on paper, 100 x 80 cm, 2008–2011, photo: Daniel Lie, © the artist

All works courtesy the artist.

Biography

Daniel Lie (they/them)
Brazilian-Indonesian, born in 1988 in São Paulo, Brazil
Lives and works in Berlin, Germany

EDUCATION

2020–19 Darmasiswa, fellowship program for traditional Indonesian dance, Indonesian Institute of Arts, Yogyakarta, Indonesia
2013 Teaching degree in Fine Arts, São Paulo State University, São Paulo, Brazil
2011 BA in Fine Arts, São Paulo State University, São Paulo

SOLO EXHIBITIONS

2021 ***Scales of Decay***, Künstlerhaus Bethanien, Berlin, Germany
2019 ***Human Supremacy: The failed project***, Casa do Povo, São Paulo
The Negative Years, Jupiter Art Land, Edinburgh, Scotland
2018 ***Children of End***, Casa Triângulo, São Paulo
2017 ***Death Center for the Living***, Wiener Festwochen, Vienna, Austria
2016 ***How low can you go?***, Change-Change, Budapest, Hungary
PODRERA, Kampnagel, Hamburg, Germany
2015 ***Lie Liong Khing***, Casa Triângulo, São Paulo
Covenant with the Future, Centro Cultural São Paulo, São Paulo
Meus Sentimentos, Oficina Cultural Oswald de Andrade, São Paulo
2011 ***Âmago***, Institute of Arts at São Paulo State University, São Paulo

GROUP EXHIBITIONS

2021 ***Park Platz***, Berlinische Galerie, Berlin, Germany
2020 ***À Construção***, Solar dos Abacaxis, Rio de Janeiro, Brazil
2018 ***Espacios Revelados***, Bucaramanga, Colombia
Valongo Festival, Santos, Brazil
Via Aérea, Sesc Belenzinho, São Paulo
Bouge B Festival, De Singel International Arts Center, Antwerp, Belgium
The sun teaches us that history is not everything, Osage Foundation, Hong Kong
2017 ***14th Yogyakarta Biennale***, Yogyakarta Nacional Museum, Yogykarta, Indonesia
Frestas – Art Triennial, Sesc Sorocaba, Sorocaba, Brazil
Welt Kompakt?, Frei_raum Q21, MuseumsQuartier, Vienna
2016 ***O que vem com a aurora***, Casa Triângulo, São Paulo
All quiet, all for the best – Projeto Brasil, Hellerau, Dresden, Germany
CCBB Música Performance 4, Centro Cultural Banco do Brasil, São Paulo
Espacios Revelados, Santiago, Chile
2015 ***34th Arte Pará***, Pará State Museum, Belém do Pará, Brazil
Abre Alas 11, A Gentil Carioca, Rio de Janeiro, Brazil

About the authors

Ruli Moretti is an independent curator, cultural manager, and editor. Since 2012, she has lived and worked in Belém, the capital city of the Brazilian state of Pará in the Amazon, from where she has organized and collaborated in both independent and institutional projects that promote the democratization of the access to arts as a means of supporting encounters and collective experience. Currently, she is investigating the role of written texts in contemporary art practices and how they operate as a specific medium with discursive and fictional possibilities of their own. In addition, Moretti has worked directly with artists in exploring, broadening, and understanding their creative processes and writing practices. For this project, she is working alongside Daniel Lie to offer curatorial support both for the exhibition *Scales of Decay* and for this publication.

Nomaduma Rosa Masilela is an artist, writer, and curator. Her work and interests center around collective work and strategy; public and performance art; ideas of the uncanny, the absurd, the dissonant; and the ambivalent natures of authenticity, history, and identity production. She holds a Masters in Art History and Philosophy from Columbia University in New York. She has written essays for various exhibition catalogs and publications, including *Blackness at MoMA* (2019), *We don't need another hero* (2018), *Portia Zvavahera: I'm with You* (2017), as well as for publications for the Studio Museum in Harlem, New York. Her curatorial practice includes exhibitions and projects with the Rijksakademie in Amsterdam, the Museum of Modern Art in New York, The Kitchen in New York, and her contributions as a co-curator of the 10th Berlin Biennale for Contemporary Art, including a curatorial publication project and reading room titled *Strange Attractors* (2018). Previous years of research focused on collective and performance art practices in Dakar, Senegal. As part of her current commitments, she is critically supporting the work of queer and femme-identifying artists from the Global South and its diasporas.

farid rakun describes himself as wearing many hats, depending on who's asking. An architect by training, he holds a B.Arch from Universitas Indonesia and an M.Arch from Cranbrook Academy of Art. In addition to his role as visiting lecturer in the Architecture Department of Universitas Indonesia, he is also a member of the artist collective ruangrupa, with whom he has permeated different artistic spaces and institutions in various contexts and geographies. Together with this collective, he co-curated TRANSaction: Sonsbeek 2016 in Arnhem, Netherlands, and currently serves as the first collective artistic director for the fifteenth edition of documenta to be held in Kassel in 2022.

Daniel Lie – Scales of Decay
With texts by Daniel Lie, a conversation with farid rakun and an essay by Nomaduma Rosa Masilela
Editors: Daniela Leykam, Christoph Tannert

Künstlerhaus Bethanien GmbH, Kohlfurter Straße 41/43, Showroom: Kottbusser Str. 10, D-10999 Berlin, www.bethanien.de
Artistic Director: Christoph Tannert / **Administrative Director:** Andrea Boche
International Studio Programme: Valeria Schulte-Fischedick / **Press & PR:** Yvonne de Andrés
Administration: Ute Werner / **Technical Staff:** Toni Lebkücher, Peter Rosemann

KfW Stiftung, Palmengartenstraße 5–9, D-60325 Frankfurt am Main, www.kfw-stiftung.de
Programme Manager Arts and Culture: Daniela Leykam

Editing: Tomke Braun, Daniela Leykam, Ruli Moretti / **Project Coordination:** Tomke Braun
Photos: Filipe Berndt, David Brandt, Ruth Clark, Edouard Fraipont, Lie Liong Khing, Daniel Lie, Leonardo Matsuhei, Martin Meiser
Proofreading: Stefan Hollstein, Aymone Rassaerts
Design: Thorsten Probst / angenehme-gestaltung.de / **Production:** Druckerei Kettler, Bönen

Published by Verlag Kettler, Dortmund, www.verlag-kettler.de

This catalogue is published on the occasion of the exhibition *Scales of Decay* by Daniel Lie, International Studio Programme, Künstlerhaus Bethanien, Berlin, 11 June 2021 to 11 July 2021. Daniel Lie is a grantholder of KfW Stiftung.

The artist would like to acknowledge Ruli Moretti for her curatorial support both for the exhibition *Scales of Decay* and for this publication, as well as Amanda Carneiro, Ana Druwe, Iranilda Elias da Costa Lie, Juliana Dos Santos.

Further publications of the book series so far: PARADISE / Thabiso Sekgala / January 2014, THE MADMAN SEES WHAT HE SEES / Carla Zaccagnini / March 2014, STORE IN A COOL AND DRY PLACE / Prajakta Potnis / November 2014, LIFE ON MARS / Stary Mwaba / March 2015, THE LAND BENEATH MY FEET / Khvay Samnang / September 2015, IN SILENCE / Nguyen Thi Thanh Mai / March 2016, INTENDING PROBABILITY / Salwa Aleryani / March 2017, AOS VENCEDORES AS BATATAS / Matheus Rocha Pitta / June 2017, EXIT – ENTRANCE / Orawan Arunrak / August 2017, ALL THAT IS SEEN AND UNSEEN / Vartan Avakian / January 2019 / FEEDING THE SCENE / Elia Nurvista / July 2019, RADIO CARABUCO / Andrés Pereira Paz / November 2019 / ... THESE GESTURES OF MEMORY / Gladys Kalichini / September 2020, MARBLE DUST / Talya Lubinsky / December 2020, CULTURA PROFILÁCTICA / Hamlet Lavastida / May 2021

ISBN 978-3-86206-946-0

KÜNSTLERHAUS BETHANIEN